BEGINNING JAZZ IMPROVISATION A

INTERMEDIATE LEVEL

LEE EVANS JAZZ
PIANO METHOD SERIES

Contents

EDWARD B. Marks Music Company

EXCLUSIVELY DISTRIBUTED BY

HAL•LEONARD® CORPORATION

7777 W. BLUEMOUND RD. P.O. BOX 13819 MILWAUKEE, WI 53213

T0050934

For all works contained herein:
Unauthorized copying, arranging, adapting, recording or public performance is an infringement of copyri
Infringers are liable under the law.

Lee Evans

Lee Evans as a professional artist has blended the performance of classical music and jazz in a most successful manner. His piano concepts and techniques have drawn much praise from audiences and fellow-musicians.

Born in New York City, Evans started private piano lessons at an early age. He graduated from New York's High School of Music and Art, then completed degrees at New York University and Columbia University, receiving his Master of Arts and Doctor of Education from the latter.

In education, he has taught at the junior high school, high school and college levels. Professionally, he plays solo piano, with his trio, and appears in the roles of pianist and music director for such performers as Engelbert Humperdinck, Tom Jones, Cat Stevens, Carol Channing, Emerson, Lake & Palmer, etc. As a featured artist, he has recorded on MGM, Command and Capitol Record labels.

Evans feels strongly that jazz techniques be taught and understood at the keyboard with the same authenticity and skill which Hanon, Czerny, and others brought to traditional teaching. He hopes these books succeed in bringing to all keyboard students and teachers this better understanding and feeling of jazz.

The Publisher

The author gratefully acknowledges the invaluable editorial assistance provided by Marcia Klebanow for this series.

General Principles for "Beginning Jazz Improvisation"

Musical improvisation is a spontaneous creation of music. In jazz, improvisation is usually accomplished within the framework of given chord patterns and melody.

First efforts at melodic improvisation should be based upon the chord arrangement of blues progression and practiced in all twelve major keys.

CHORD PATTERNS:

12 Bar Blues Progression in C Major:

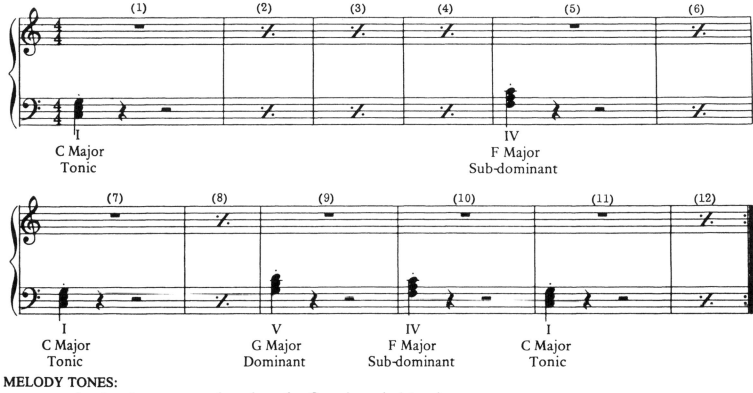

MELODY TONES:

In the above example, when the C major triad (tonic triad) is played by the left hand, right hand melodic improvisation should use a combination of these chord tones:

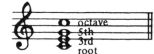

and these blues scale tones: (Lowered 3rd, 5th and 7th degrees of a major scale are called *blue notes* in jazz. The formula for the blues scale, derived from the major scale, follows.)

(Blues Scale in C Major)

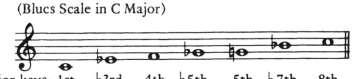

Formula for blues scale in all major keys: 1st ♭3rd 4th ♭5th 5th ♭7th 8th

for a total of the following tones:

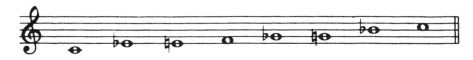

Copyright © 1980 by Piedmont Music Company
Sole Selling Agent: Edward B. Marks Music Company
International Copyright Secured   All Rights Reserved   Used by Permission

4

Similarly, when the F major triad (sub-dominant triad) is played by the left hand, the following combination of chord tones and blues scale tones should be used:

When the G major triad (dominant triad) is played by the left hand, the following combination of chord tones and blues scale tones should be used:

An infinite variety of rhythms may be employed in improvisation. It is suggested, however, that initially the rhythms of some of the exercises appearing in the book "Keyboard Jazz - The Elements of Jazz" be utilized.

Rhythm Patterns:

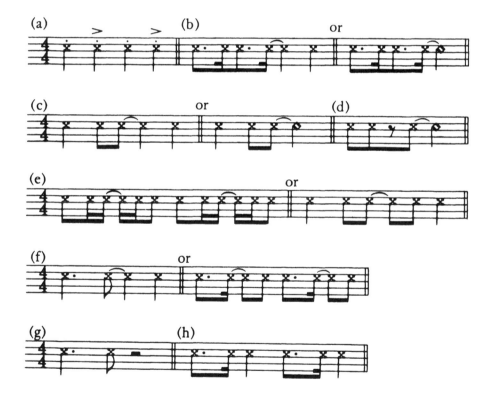

All rights reserved, including rights of reproduction and use in any form or by any means, including the making of copies by any photo process, or by any electronic or mechanical device, printed, written or oral, or recording for sound or visual reproduction or for use in any information storage and retrieval system or device, unless permission in writing is obtained from the copyright proprietors.

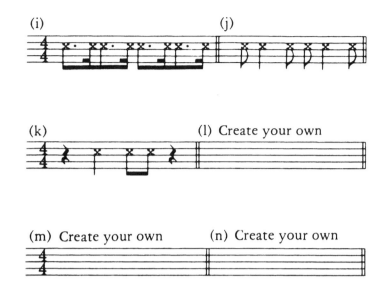

Beginning Jazz Improvisation
(Blue Notes)

I. One Blues Scale Tone

At first, the student should attempt to use only *one blues scale tone* (♭3) in combination with chord tones:

applying *one or two of the aforementioned rhythm patterns* to those tones. For example:

Improvisational Example:

Bass pattern (built on the tonic triad of the major scale).

Now improvise your own right hand with the given bass pattern, using chord tones, the flatted third, and any one or two rhythm patterns from pages 4 or 5.

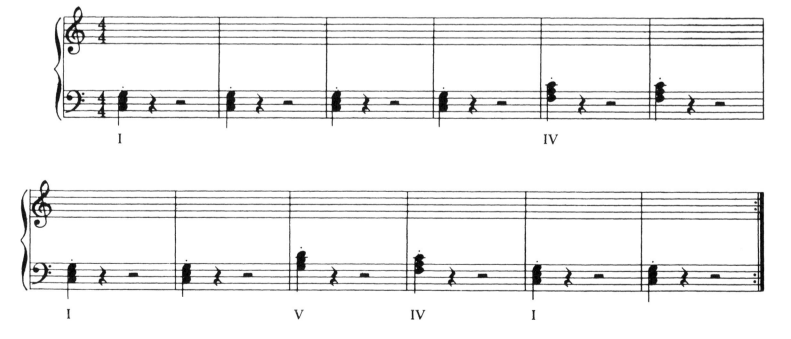

Using the *same* improvisation you have created, substitute a *walking bass* built on the 8th, 7th, 6th and 5th degrees of the major scale. In a walking bass, the left hand imitates the string bass, one note per count and usually in stepwise motion:

Example:

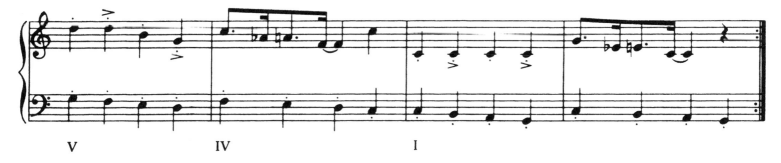

Apply your own improvisation here:

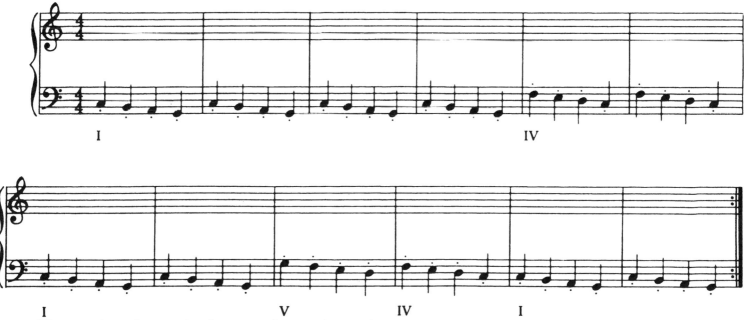

The previous improvisation exercises, using only one blue note in combination with chord tones, should be attempted in several different keys --- creating a new improvisation each time.

II. Two Blues Scale Tones

Improvise a different melody with any one or two different rhythm patterns on pages 4 or 5, combining chord tones with *two* blues scale tones (♭3 and ♭5).

Example:

New bass pattern (built on the tonic and dominant tones of the major scale)

Now improvise your own:

The above improvisation exercise, using two blue notes in combination with chord tones, **should be attempted in several different keys --- creating a new improvisation each time.**

III. Three Blues Scale Tones

Improvise a new melody with any one or two of the rhythm patterns on pages 4 and 5, combining chord tones with *three* blues scale tones (♭3, ♭5, ♭7).

Example:

New bass pattern (built on the tonic of the major scale)

Now improvise your own:

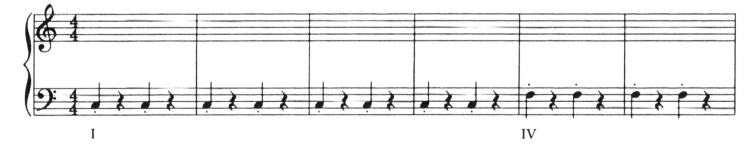

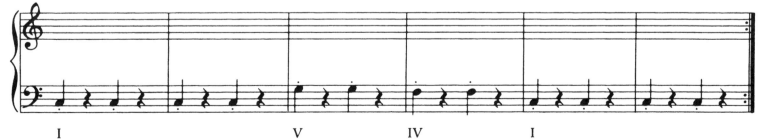

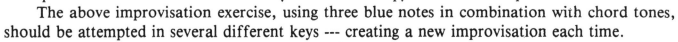

The above improvisation exercise, using three blue notes in combination with chord tones, should be attempted in several different keys --- creating a new improvisation each time.

IV. Walking Bass with Blues Scale Tone

Introduce a blues scale tone into a walking bass, and create a new improvisation, using any combination of chord tones, blues scale tones, and rhythm patterns.

Example:

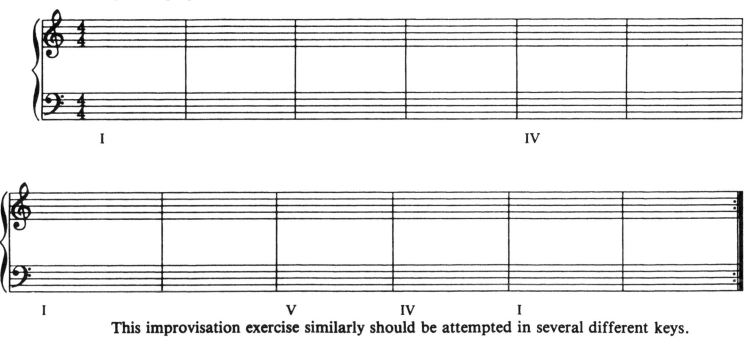

Now create your own walking bass (using at least one blues scale tone), and improvise your own melody to be played with it.

This improvisation exercise similarly should be attempted in several different keys.

Improvisation Using Boogie-Woogie Patterns *(based upon blues progression)*

Boogie-woogie is an ostinato (a short, constantly repeated musical phrase) left-hand bass figure against which the right hand improvises freely. Students should try to improvise a right-hand melody using given boogie-woogie bass patterns (in all keys). Right-hand improvisations should employ chord tones and blue notes from the blues scale (see page 3). In terms of melodic rhythms, refer to all previous rhythm patterns in this book as source material.

The effective use of grace notes, trills, quartal harmony, etc., is shown in the book "Keyboard Jazz - The Elements of Jazz" and these devices may be incorporated in further improvisational attempts.

Example:

Create your own improvisation:

1.

Create additional improvisations using these two different boogie-woogie bass patterns:

2.

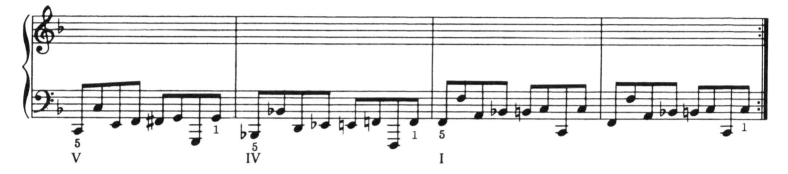

Improvisation from a Lead Sheet

Jazz musicians must learn to improvise from *lead sheets,* which generally consist of a single melody line with chord symbols. Lead sheets are found in *fake books,* so-called because "fake" is synonymous with "improvise" in the jazz language. What has to be "faked," or improvised, with the given melody and chord symbols are bass line (accompaniment), and melodic development in the appropriate style.

Example of a typical lead sheet:

The basic chords to be used in the following improvisation are:

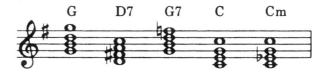

Example of a jazz improvisation based on the above lead sheet:

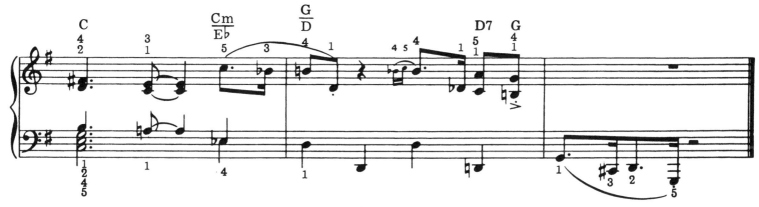

In the preceding arrangement, note the use of such jazz characteristics as:

1. grace note; two grace notes; grace note embellishing the bottom tone of the chord that follows.
2. rhythmic and melodic alteration of the given melody.
3. walking bass
4. blue notes
5. accents on offbeats
6. syncopated rhythms
7. detached style of playing
8. seventh chord
9. trill
10. anticipation
11. delay

On the next page, using some or all of the jazz elements listed above, create your own jazz improvisation based on the following lead sheet:

Auld Lang Syne

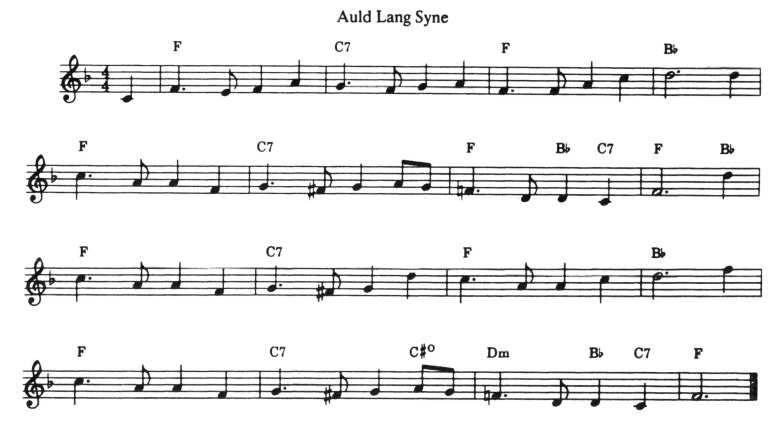

The basic chords in·the above lead sheet and the following improvisation are:

Auld Lang Syne

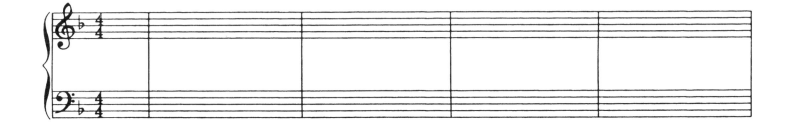

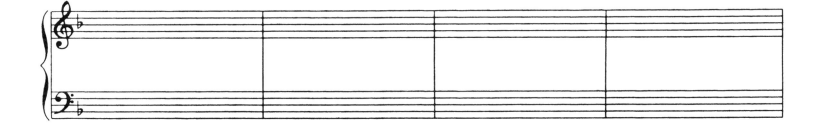

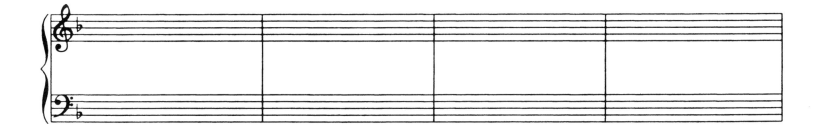

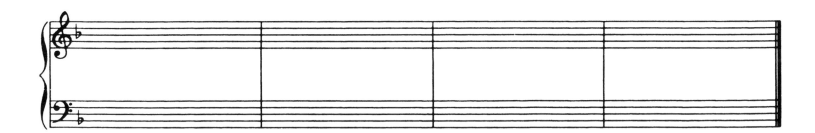